The Airsoft Question a

Author: Paul Love

Contact Information

Email address: ioxbooks@gmail.com

PREFACE

If you're a parent with a youngster who's suddenly become interested in airsoft guns or you've got a friend who's trying to talk you into joining his airsoft team or you've heard about airsoft and just want a better idea of what it is, this book can help answer some of your questions. "The Airsoft Question and Answer Book" isn't intended to cover everything about airsoft or to make you an expert at playing in airsoft games, but it can give a good overview of the sport.

Before you get into specific questions, a quick introduction to airsoft may be helpful. Simply put, airsoft is a shooting sport that makes use of guns that are replicas of real pistols and rifles and fire 6 millimeter plastic BBs. Airsoft guns can be powered by a spring, by gas, or by batteries and shoot BBs at speeds from 100 fps (feet per second) up to 500 fps or more. Why are airsoft guns becoming so popular? Some people collect them simply because they're almost exact replicas of real firearms; others buy them because airsoft guns provide a safe, low cost way to practice shooting skills at home with a weapon that's virtually identical to an actual firearm.

However, more and more people (of all ages) are buying airsoft guns and equipment in order to take part in airsoft game playing. Airsoft matches are generally military simulations played by two teams either in indoor facilities or outdoors in a woodland setting. Airsoft guns used in game play are limited to a certain range of muzzle velocities - powerful enough to raise a welt if a BB fired at close range hits an opponent on his bare skin, but not strong enough to penetrate skin or cause any serious damage. The only real danger in being hit by an airsoft BB is if you're hit in the eye or mouth and virtually all regulated airsoft courses have strict rules about wearing adequate eye and face protection.

You may have seen or heard about young kids running around a neighborhood shooting at each other with airsoft guns and, in many cases, without wearing any protection. Everyone who's actually involved in the sport recognizes the potential dangers involved in these "backyard airsoft" games and supports efforts to make sure that kids who have been given airsoft guns get adult supervision. If at all possible, youngsters should be taken to play at authorized airsoft fields where they can be taught how to play the game safely and according to a standard set of rules.

Who exactly plays airsoft games and why do they do it? If you go to a typical airsoft match you're liable to see players ranging in age from 14 or 15 to 50 or older, both men and women. Accountants, sales people, students, construction workers, soldiers and ex-soldiers -- players come from all walks of life. They play because of the comraderie, the chance to practice military skills, the opportunity to get some exercise and have fun at the same time, and for the challenge of working out tactics that will help defeat their opponents.

So, whether you're interested in collecting airsoft guns, using them to sharpen your shooting skills or thinking about joining a team, here's a chance to learn some of the basics of airsoft. Take some time and browse through the questions and answers inside for a more detailed look at the sport.

Table of Contents

Airsoft in General

What is airsoft?

Basically airsoft is a rapidly growing pastime involving BB guns that shoot "soft" plastic BBs, allowing kids (and adults) to play out military or law-enforcement style games using realistic equipment and scenarios. It can be as simple as some kids running around in a back yard for a few hours shooting at each other or as complicated as a large group of older players carrying out a full "milsim" (military simulation) exercise that can last for several days. In some cases airsoft replica guns are also used by both the police and military for training purposes, providing an easy and inexpensive alternative to other training methods.

How did airsoft guns get started?

Airsoft originated in Japan in the 1970s, beginning with 1:1 scale model plastic replicas of popular firearms. These kits quickly led to production of cap gun and spring-driven pellet gun versions of these replicas. The cap gun versions didn't do anything except make a loud bang and they never really caught on. Spring powered BB guns (in a country where possession of real firearms is banned) did catch on - in a big way.

Early models (most of which were made to resemble semi-automatic pistols) featured soft plastic "bullets" that were inserted in a plastic shell similar to a regular firearm cartridge. The cartridges were then loaded into a magazine which was inserted into the pistol. Racking the pistol's slide pulled a cartridge into the firing chamber and compressed a spring. Pulling the trigger released the spring, driving a piston forward which went through the hollow rear end of the shell, firing the bullet out the barrel of the pistol. At the same time the slide moved toward the rear and the empty shell casing was ejected, just like a real pistol. The plastic "bullets" were hard to find and expensive and were soon replaced by round BBs, which were much easier to manufacture. Also, it was a real hassle to collect the ejected "shells" every time and before long the shells were done away with entirely, leaving just the plastic

BBs.

In the 1980s Daisy made an effort to market similar BB guns (called "Replisoft" or "soft air" guns), using the plastic shell and BB design. These spring guns never quite gained popularity in the U.S. and were discontinued a few years later. By the 1990s though, airsoft guns imported from Asia started getting a foothold in the United States and the airsoft market began a steady growth (even enticing Daisy to re-enter the airsoft market in 2003).

Are BBs and pellets the same thing?

Technically the term "BBs" should be used to mean the metal ammunition that's used in a regular air pistol or rifle; and the term "pellets" should be used to mean the lead pellets used in high-powered air pistols and rifles. Originally, airsoft ammunition was referred to as "plastic pellets"; however, most airsofters use the word "BBs" when they talk about the 6mm plastic pellets used in airsoft guns. For the sake of simplicity then, this book will always refer to airsoft ammunition as "BBs".

Is it safe for kids (or adults) to play airsoft?

Airsoft games are reasonably safe if players use proper eye protection (goggles or masks) and guns that have muzzle velocities below 400 feet per second. If you're hit by a BB at close range you may get a welt, but the light weight and low energy of the plastic BBs used in airsoft guns makes them much safer than metal BBs. Keep in mind though that any BB that hits you in the face could possibly do some minor damage, such as a chipped tooth. To be safe it's best to wear a full face mask rather than just goggles.

NOTE: A few airsoft fields require ear protection. A stocking cap, helmet, or even a balaclava can cover your ears sufficiently to meet that requirement, although some players may opt for a full paintball mask with eye and ear protection. Most airsoft players don't wear any ear protection and there doesn't seem to be any evidence of serious injuries involving player's ears. One thing to keep in mind is that if you do wear something over your ears, make sure it doesn't fit so closely it interferes with your hearing - the ability to hear everything going on around you is essential in game play.

Another thing to consider is that even airsoft BBs can crack a window or make a hole in a piece of drywall. Outdoors, avoid shooting in the direction of a house or any other structure. Indoors, it's a good idea to hang some tarps or blankets on the walls to prevent scratches, broken light bulbs, or damaged paneling.

There are also some safety factors that involve your airsoft gun. All airsoft guns sold in the U.S. are required to have a bright orange tip on the end of the barrel so they can't be mistaken for a real firearm. At times the plastic tip may break off or if the end of the barrel is simply painted orange, the paint may wear off. In either case you should try to keep the orange tip intact if you're going to be taking the gun anywhere outside your house. You should also be sure you have a working safety on your gun and keep in on when it's not being used (and keep your gun unloaded when you store it).

And finally, if you use a gas gun, don't leave it in direct sun on hot day with gas in it. The propane or CO_2 can overheat and actually explode. The same thing of course goes for cans of green gas or propane or a box of CO_2 powerlets.

What are some reasons to take up airsoft?
Airsoft provides many of the benefits of taking part in any sport -- good physical exercise, the thrill of competition, camaraderie, and experience in working as part of a team. In addition airsoft gaming helps develop the ability to work out the tactics and strategy necessary to achieve your goal. Plus, if you can't run a four-minute mile or dunk a basketball you can still take part in an airsoft competition - and it can be a great way to relieve stress. If nothing else, airsoft (whether target shooting or actual game competition) at least gets you out and away from the TV.

Also, for young people who may end up in the military, airsoft may offer one benefit more important than any of those above. The things you learn now that help you to survive in an airsoft game may be the very things that help you survive in combat in the future.

Do airsoft games promote violence?

There are always going to be differing opinions about this. However, long before airsoft, kids played games that involved sword fights or shooting at each other with cap pistols and it's doubtful that those generations produced any more than their share of violent people.   And you could also argue that supervised airsoft games offer a good way for youngsters to work off some energy while learning to work together as a team.

What are some of the differences between paintball and airsoft?

Both paintball and airsoft competitions offer some of the same benefits, but paintball (in general) is more of a straight-up shooting match, while airsoft games, other than the neighborhood variety, tend to focus more on realistic situations, weapons and equipment. Also, unless you're playing "woodsball" paintball, airsoft games usually emphasize tactics a little more than paintball. Moneywise, airsoft equipment can be considerably less expensive than paintball gear, just depending on how much you want to spend.

Do paintballs hit harder than airsoft BBs?

A typical paintball weighing about 3 grams and traveling at 300 feet per second will transfer about 12 joules of energy on impact, while most airsoft BBs transfer about 1 joule of energy - considerably less than a paintball. Of course if you're hit at close range by an airsoft BB traveling at higher speed (say 450 - 500 fps) there will be more energy transferred, but paintballs are so much more massive that they're going to hit harder in almost all cases.

Can airsoft guns help you to learn to use a real firearm?

The short answer is yes - to some extent. Airsoft pistols and rifles are often almost exact replicas of real firearms, from the gun's size and weight right down to the location and function of the various controls like safeties, mag release buttons, and slide locks. And if you have a "blowback" airsoft gun you can definitely get the feel of handling a firearm. Of course the noise level and strength of recoil are (generally) much less, but an airsoft gun is also a whole lot safer and less expensive to use while learning how to handle a firearm. One other item to note is that while a "blowback" airsoft gun tends to be less accurate than a non-blowback gun, it's very useful in getting you used to compensating for the recoil of a real pistol or rifle.

What do airsoft guns cost?

Prices range from around $20 (for a cheap but usable spring pistol) up to a thousand dollars or more for top of the line rifles. Airsoft guns sold at discount stores tend to be at the low end of the spectrum, but there are numerous online sites that offer a wide variety of guns of different types and price ranges. In general, even the top quality spring pistols are under $50, while the best spring-powered sniper rifles run up to several hundred dollars. Most gas pistols (including green gas, propane and CO2 pistols) run from around $40 up to $200 or more. AEG (Automatic Electric Guns) go for somewhere in the range of $80 to $500 or more.

How much does it cost to play airsoft at an airsoft field?

Most airsoft fields charge between twenty and forty dollars a day. There may also be an additional charge if you need to rent any equipment (AEG, goggles or face mask, vest, etc.).

Are airsoft games only for kids?

Actually, the majority of organized airsoft games include people from teenagers to adults of all ages (both men and women). High school and college students, bankers, bakers, construction workers, accountants, soldiers and ex-soldiers - people from all walks of life take part in airsofting these days.

Why do adults get involved in airsoft?

If you want to recapture your childhood or relive your time in the military, airsoft gaming could be the answer. It's an inexpensive hobby that allows you to get together with some friends, practice your marksmanship and see if you can outwit the "opposing force".

Do colleges have airsoft teams?
Many colleges and universities have airsoft teams. Just to name a few: Kansas State University, Florida Atlantic University, Clemson, Michigan University, Purdue, West Point, Georgia Tech, Connecticut University, and the University of Texas (2 campuses).

How popular is airsoft?
It's popular enough that in places like the Philippines, the scores of organized airsoft games are reported in local papers just like any other sporting event. And if you search the internet for airsoft forums you'll find dozens of them, some with hundreds of members. Maybe the best indicator of the growing popularity of airsoft is the increasing number of web sites selling airsoft guns, BBs and other equipment.

What type of ammunition does an airsoft gun use?
Almost all airsoft guns use 6 millimeter plastic BBs, but there are different weights of airsoft BBs (.12 gram, .20 gram, .23 gram, .25 gram, etc.) and different types of guns work best with different weights. Cheaper, low-powered guns normally use .12g BBs -- they provide the highest muzzle velocity, but due to their light weight, they tend to be the least accurate. Outdoors especially, .12g BBs are greatly affected by the wind at all but very close distances. The most commonly used BBs are .2 grams, although higher powered electric and spring rifles usually perform better with .25 gram, .28 gram, or even heavier BBs. There are also metal (aluminum) airsoft BBs that weigh around .30 grams, but these should only be used for target practice, never for airsoft games.

How fast do airsoft BBs travel?
Most airsoft guns shoot 0.2 gram BBs at speeds from about 100 fps (feet per second) for a low-powered spring pistol up to around 500 fps or more for customized sniper rifles. The majority of AEGs or Automatic Electric Guns (the main weapon for most airsofters) produce speeds from 250 fps to 400 fps.

Is airsoft bad for the environment?
The major issue with airsoft is the potential damage to the environment from thousands of plastic BBs scattered around.

For outdoor games players should use bio-degradable BBs. They may take years to actually dissolve but new versions that decay faster (and perform better) are becoming available and they are at least somewhat less potentially damaging to the environment.

Are there any places in the U.S. where airsoft guns are illegal?
Currently, airsoft guns are illegal in New York City (all five boroughs), Washington D.C., San Francisco and portions of Michigan.

What are the different types of airsoft guns?
Categories of airsoft guns include: sidearms, PDWs (Personal Defense Weapons), CQB (Close Quarters Battle) weapons, assault rifles, sniper and battle rifles, squad weapons and machine guns.

Sidearms include pistols of various types: spring powered, electric, and gas powered. If you're an airsoft player you should have a sidearm as a backup weapon. Exactly what kind is a matter of choice; springers are durable and reliable (no gas or batteries to deal with) but they have to be cocked for every shot which gives them a low rate of fire and tends to decrease accuracy (since you have to reacquire your target each time you cock the pistol). Electric pistols are generally very low-powered and tend to break fairly easily. Gas pistols (powered by CO_2, propane, or other types of gas) are affected by colder weather and some CO_2 powered models are too powerful for airsoft play; however gas pistols are semi-automatic or fully automatic which gives them a high rate of fire and many of them are accurate out to 125 feet or more.

NOTE: With the exception of most sniper rifles (which are usually spring-powered), the other guns listed below are all classified as AEGs (Automatic Electric Guns).

PDWs (Personal Defense Weapons) are compact, semi or fully automatic weapon, which bridge the categories of sidearm and CQB (Close Quarters Battle) gun. Airsoft PDWs can range from 300 fps or 320 fps muzzle velocity up to 400 fps, with an effective range of about 120 to 130 feet. With a folding stock, a PDW can be carried almost as easily as a pistol. Galaxy's MK5 and Echo 1's Task Force are examples of current airsoft PDW weapons.

If you're going to be playing both CQB (Close Quarters Battle) and open or woodland skirmishing, there are a number of airsoft guns that fall into the CQB category that will work for either type of game. The M4 carbine, MP5, G36, and P90 are some of the possible choices for CQB weapons. CQB guns are more compact than regular rifles and carbines, which makes them better suited to combat in tight spaces where maneuverability is vital. Airsoft shotguns are sometimes used in CQB as well, primarily for room clearing operations.

Assault rifles (including both rifles and carbines) are replicas of the small-arms weapons issued to combat troops in many countries. They provide longer range and accuracy than CQB guns and include the M16, XM8, G36, AK-47, and M4.

Sniper and Battle rifles are long distance weapons used in open area and woodland games. These weapons are generally longer and bulkier than most airsoft guns; they're used primarily by snipers and may be single shot or semi-automatic/automatic weapons. Popular airsoft versions of sniper rifles include the M14 (last of the so-called "battle rifles"), the VSR-10 and the L96. Most of these rifles also have mounts for a telescopic sight for increased long range accuracy.

The final category of airsoft guns is the machine gun - heavy duty portable automatic weapons with high capacity magazines, designed to provide suppressing or covering fire. Their size and weight makes them a poor choice as a CQB or individual weapon, but they are an important part of base defense or for protecting team members. Airsoft machine guns include the M249 Squad Automatic Weapon (SAW) and the M60. Airsoft guns in this category are generally expensive, averaging $300 and up.

Is there an age limit for buying airsoft guns?
Yes, you have to be 18 or older to purchase airsoft guns in the U.S., with various age limits in other countries. There may also be additional restrictions depending on where you live. For example, airsoft guns (as of this writing) are considered firearms in Australia and you need a license to purchase one.

Were airguns ever used in the past for military training?
Air guns have been used a number of times in the past as a simple and inexpensive way of training troops. During World War II, the U.S. taught aerial gunnery with the aid of full-auto BB guns that resembled the Browning machine guns in use at that time. And during Vietnam, modified Daisy BB guns were employed to teach the "quick fire" snap-shooting techniques needed in close combat situations.

So are airsoft games just good physical exercise?
Properly played, airsoft games can be more than just an enjoyable way to get some physical exercise; they can also be a way to exercise your mind, to work on planning and out-thinking your opponent. For example, figuring out the best way to deploy your team for an effective ambush, with proper fields of fire and additional plans depending on how the situation develops. In the long run, learning the mental skills involved will probably be much more beneficial than the physical part of airsoft gaming.

Airsoft Guns, Gear and Ammo

What are AEGs?
AEGs (or Automatic Electric Guns) are powered by batteries and use an electric motor to drive a gear-piston system that actually fires the BBs. AEGs are the main weapon of choice for airsoft players due to combination of range, rate of fire, number of rounds per battery charge, BB capacity and faithful duplication of actual firearms. Some of the most popular models of AEGs are those that are replicas of the M4 carbine (standard issue weapon for U.S. combat forces), the M16 rifle (standard issue for U.S. forces outside of combat troops), the M14 rifle (as a sniper rifle), and other popular police and military weapons such as the MP5 submachine gun.

AEG muzzle velocities average somewhere in the neighborhood of 300-350 fps and fire at around 500-700 rounds per minute. In a standard AEG, the motor drives a series of gears inside a gearbox and the gears compress a piston assembly against a spring. When the piston is released (by pulling the trigger) the spring drives it forward, pushing a BB into the firing chamber, through the barrel, and out the muzzle.

Some of the most popular makers of AEGs are Tokyo Marui (Japan), Classic Army (Hong Kong) and ICS (Taiwan).

What do I need to know about my AEG battery?
Most AEGs use a battery pack containing either Nickel Cadmium or Nickel Metal Hydride cells (usually 7 or 8 cells per pack). Ni-cad cells are less expensive than Ni-MH cells and less likely to suffer damage from overcharging. The downside for Nickel Cadmium cells is that they need to be used regularly and if they're repeatedly overcharged they start to discharge very quickly. It's also a good idea to discharge a Ni-Cad cell completely before re-charging.

The average AEG battery will be 8.5 volts. Larger batteries are available (up to about 10.8 volts) but are intended for upgraded AEGs. Putting a 10.8 volt battery in your stock AEG will definitely increase the power, but it will also shorten the life of your gun considerably. Also the milliamp (mAh) rating of the battery is important; the higher the mAh rating, the longer the battery will last. Keep in mind though, higher milliamp batteries will also cost more.

The best chargers to use with your battery pack are voltage peak or Delta peak chargers, which monitor the pack voltage during charging. Peak chargers can detect when the pack is fully charged, avoiding overcharging situations. It's important to make sure that the charger you buy is designed for the type of cells you're using (Ni-Cad or Nickel Metal Hydride) to ensure the charger works correctly with your battery pack. An additional benefit with peak chargers is that they work much faster than other types, typically recharging an AEG battery pack in one or two hours.

Generally speaking, the time required to charge a totally discharged battery will be equal to the milliamp rating of the battery divided by the milliamp rating of your charger.

How much and what kind of maintenance do airsoft guns require?
Airsoft guns need very little upkeep compared to real firearms. On spring pistols and rifles the spring chamber and piston should be lubricated with a few drops of synthetic oil every 500 shots or so. Various other points like hinges should be lubed occasionally according to the manufacturer's instructions. Roughly every 1000 shots the barrel should be cleaned to remove any oil and dirt buildup, and treated with a light (very light) coat of silicon oil.

For CO_2 guns, the main thing to remember is to place a drop of oil on the seal and needle where the CO_2 powerlet goes. As A rule, you can just place a drop of the upper (small) end of the CO_2 cartridge before you load it into the gun.

NOTE: You should avoid "dry-firing" any spring-powered gun (that is, firing it without a BB in the chamber. The BB cushions

15

the impact of the piston and repeated dry-firing can damage the gun.

What is "hop-up"?
Many airsoft guns now include "hop-up", a device that puts backspin on the BB as it's fired. This backspin (an application of Bernoulli's principle) makes the air on top of the BB move slightly faster than the air under it and creates a small amount of lift (similar to the air flow on airplane's wing). The extra lift can add as much as 50% to the range of the gun. Of course the hop-up mechanism can produce too much lift (causing the BB to float too far upward) or too little lift (causing the BB to nose down into the ground prematurely). If possible you want to get a gun that has an adjustable hop-up mechanism so you can increase or reduce the amount of backspin put on the BB.

What's the best AEG I can buy for under $100?
If you search the most popular airsoft forums, most airsoft players will say that there aren't any AEGs under $100 that are really worth having. Best bets (currently) in the $100 range seem to be the JG KP5 A4, Galaxy MK5 PDW, and the CYMA CM028 AK47.

What's a "G36"?
Refers to the Heckler & Koch G36 Airsoft Assault Rifle; a compact AEG that's a popular weapon for airsofters. Originally introduced in the German army, it has gained worldwide use by law enforcement agencies.

What exactly is the difference between an "AEG" and an "LPEG"?
LPEGs (Low Power Electric Guns) first appeared as mini-guns - small size copies of AEGs. They were cheaply made, under-powered, and were basically just a toy. After a while some manufacturers began putting the guts of an LPEG into AEG-sized bodies and marketing them as very inexpensive AEGs. Over the years however, newer models of LPEGs have been released that are built with better materials, perform better and are much more durable. The line between AEGs and LPEGs is becoming less clear all the time, but the main differences right

now are price (LPEGs generally run under $100), quality of construction (LPEGs have plastic gearboxes and/or gears) and power (most LPEGs have muzzle velocities of 250 fps or less with .12 gram BBs compared to 280 fps or better for AEGs).

What is a "rail" on an airsoft gun?

A "rail" is a mounting system for airsoft accessories such as scopes, flashlights, and bipods; it can be built into the frame of the gun or it may be a separate attachment. It consists of a ridged piece of metal with perpendicular slots cut into it. Scopes and other items are mounted using "rings" that either slide onto the rail or are attached using bolts or thumbscrews. There are two main types of rail systems commonly used on airsoft guns: Weaver and Picatinny. Weaver rails (named after William Weaver) and Picatinny rails (named after the Picatinny Arsenal) both provide the same functionality, the only difference being the spacing between the slots cut into the rail. Any accessory that will fit on a Weaver rail will fit on a Picatinny rail, but not necessarily the other way around.

What types of sights are used on airsoft guns?

The simplest and most common type of sights are "open sights" -- basically just two pieces of metal, one toward the rear of the gun and one near the front. The rear sight is usually a "U" or "V" shape, while the front sight is just an upright metal blade; you aim by looking through the notch of the rear sight and centering the top of the front sight on your target. The rear sight may or may not be adjustable to allow for windage and elevation.

There are also various types of optical sights such as telescopic sights and reflex sights (red dot and laser scopes). Telescopic scopes are just that; magnifying devices that bring your target "up close". A "red dot" sight is basically a tube with a light-emitting diode at the near end and a metallic mirror at the far end. The mirror reflects red light only, letting all other light from the diode pass through; the reflected red light is only visible to the shooter and appears as a red dot that you can center on your target. Laser sights emit a beam of light (usually red or green) that provides a quick aiming point for short to medium range shots. Red light is best for indoors or low light, green works best outdoors or in bright light.

Another useful item that attaches like a scope is the tactical flashlight. In low-light situations a gun-mounted flashlight can serve to illuminate targets while leaving your hands free.

Does it harm an airsoft gun to dry-fire it?
The internal mechanism of both spring and electric guns work somewhat the same and can suffer damage over time by repeated dry-firing (firing the gun without any BBs in it). Both types of guns have a piston that drives forward against the BB, compressing the air behind the BB and propelling the BB out the barrel. If there's no BB in the cylinder to cushion the piston, the piston slams into the end of the cylinder harder then it normally would. The additional impact that dry firing your gun constantly causes will definitely decrease the life of your weapon (and in some cheaper models dry firing even a few times can ruin the gun).

Can airsoft guns be upgraded?
Some airsoft guns (particularly certain AEGs) can be upgraded to increase muzzle velocity or to improve durability. Bigger batteries and stronger springs are available for some AEGs; while these upgrades provide more power, they also tend to shorten the life of the gun since the power boost puts more strain on the internal parts of the AEG. Upgraded barrels are also available for particular AEG models and can improve overall performance.

AEG gearboxes usually contain some plastic parts -- replacing the gearbox with one that has all metal parts can extend the life of the gun considerably, to as much as double it's normal lifespan.

Are there any spring guns that can compete with AEGs?
There are only a few spring powered guns (other than sniper rifles) that are usable in airsoft games. One of the best known is the UHC MP5 SD3 is a spring powered gun that outperforms most LPEGs (Low Powered Electric Guns).

What about airsoft shotguns?
Shotguns can be a good choice for airsoft gaming, due to their combination of power and accuracy. There are versions ranging from double-barreled to multi-shot tactical shotguns, and they're available in spring-powered, pump, and gas powered versions. Spring powered shotguns are less expensive but pump shotguns offer considerably more power. You also have a choice between pistol grip models and full stock shotguns; which one you choose is pretty much a matter of personal preference, but if accuracy is important the full stock versions have the edge.

Do I need special clothing or equipment to play airsoft games?
Most airsoft fields don't require anything special other than adequate eye protection. However most players end up buying military clothing and gear in order to look as realistic as possible and to provide extra protection. Military surplus stores are often a good source for affordable clothing such as BDUs (Battle Dress Uniforms), helmets, backpacks, web belts and canteens. Tactical vests are a good investment too and reasonably priced ones can be found online. A decent vest can include a holster, pockets for spare magazines and Co2 and additional pockets for miscellaneous items. You may want to get a pair of airsoft gloves (the fingerless variety) as well; they can protect your hands and help you keep a firm grip on your weapon even if your hands are cold or sweaty. Most airsoft players also wear boots and you can find inexpensive ones at Walmart, Kmart or other discount stores. And finally, miscellaneous items that may come in handy include kneepads, a gear bag, a flashlight, a rifle sling, and a multi-tool of some type for emergency repairs. Regardless of whether you buy military type clothing or equipment, you should always wear a long-sleeved shirt and long pants to keep BBs from hitting you on bare skin.

What is "body armor"?
Many airsoft players wear "body armor"; light-weight airsoft vests that contain small plastic plates that protect the body. Body armor is also popular because it resembles actual body armor worn by combat troops, which increases the feeling of

realism in an airsoft game.

What is a bipod?
A bipod or tripod is a stabilizing device that's either permanently attached or can be mounted on the front of a rifle. In airsoft competitions, bipods are really only of use to snipers or other long range shooters, to help steady the weapon.

What is a "suppressor" or "silencer" and do I need one?
A suppressor (also referred to as a "silencer") is a device attached to the barrel of a firearm to reduce the flash and noise when a round is fired. Airsoft suppressors are for just for looks and to change the sound the gun makes when it fires. Suppressors don't affect range, accuracy or noise level of an airsoft gun in any significant way. One reason you might want one though (aside from looks) would be to protect the inner barrel of your gun.

What special types of weapons are used in airsoft games?
In addition to pistols, rifles and submachine guns, modern airsoft weapons also include grenades, grenade launchers, and mines. For example, you can buy an airsoft version of the M72 Light Anti-tank Weapon (LAW), which fires standard M203 gas BB shower shells. And if you look around on the internet you can also find information on how to make your airsoft "mortars", and other similar items. By the way, a lot of these "explosive devices" are filled with things like dried peas or nerf balls -- nothing that could be dangerous. Even so, many airsoft fields don't allow these types of weapons (or they place limits on the amount of smoke, flash, or noise that these items can produce).

What's a "trip" mine?
A trip mine is a mine that can be set up to be detonated by triggering a trip wire attached to the mine. For example, you can buy airsoft "claymore" mines that operate with either with a remote control or a trip wire. Airsoft mines usually are spring powered, reusable, and fire a burst of BBs up to 30 or 40 feet.

Can you buy airsoft grenades?

Yes, there are reusable airsoft grenades. You fill them with gas (usually green gas) and a large number of BBs (200 BBs for most models). There's a timer that you can set to give yourself several seconds to throw the grenade once the pin is pulled; then the gas fires the BBs out in all directions. Better quality grenades of this type can run from 50 to 100 dollars or more. CAUTION: these ready-made airsoft grenades seem to work pretty well when they work -- however there are a lot of reviews on the internet indicating that they malfunction a good deal of the time and tend to break easily.

Can you buy smoke grenades?
You can get smoke grenades from fireworks stores and paintball supply stores. They are inexpensive, put out a nice cloud of white smoke that lasts for 15 seconds or more, and really come in handy if you need to try to blind enemy troops for a few seconds. Smoke grenades can also be used to signal other members of your team by using grenades of different colors. For example, if you and a teammate are trapped and about to be overrun by enemy troops you could set off a red smoke grenade to let other members of your team know where you are and that you need help. Keep in mind though that a lot of airsoft fields don't allow the use of any pyrotechnics.

What kinds of airsoft targets are available?
The most common type of airsoft target is the "sticky target" made of gel foam. It works fairly well for lower powered guns (those with a muzzle velocity of around 300 feet per second or less). The idea is that the BB hits the gel foam and sticks there (temporarily at least) and then slowly slides down and drops into a tray beneath the target. The BBs can then be collected easily and possibly re-used. The downside of gel foam targets is that the BB can bounce off the target or hit and drop down into the tray before you can tell where it hit.

There are several other types of targets, including those with moving parts to shoot at and those with a paper target backed by a net to trap the BBs after they pass through the target. There are also blocks of foam with targets printed on them, which trap the BBs inside the foam block.

And of course there are home-made targets: cardboard boxes filled with newspaper, pop cans, balloons, and so forth. All of these can make work just as well as commercial products, although they tend to work best outdoors where you don't have to police up BBs that have rolled under furniture or other obstacles.

What's an "ACOG" sight?
An ACOG (Advanced Combat Optical Gunsight) is a telescopic sight.

What is a "battery box"?
Battery boxes are used on AEGs (Automatic Electric Guns) and are usually disguised as some kind of tactical accessory. They are used to house the battery for the AEG and provide easy access if you want to swap the battery out for a fresh one.

What do you use to lubricate an airsoft gun?
Use a non-petroleum based silicon lubricant that won't harm the rubber and plastic parts of your airsoft gun. Most of the silicon lubricants you can get at the hardware store contain petroleum products that will eventually destroy plastic parts. WD-40 and similar products will also damage airsoft guns. Check at your local airsoft store or at an online airsoft dealer to make sure you can the proper lubricant.

What parts of my airsoft gun need lubrication?
There are a number of parts on your pistol, rifle or AEG that should be lubricated periodically to help prevent excessive wear and tear. A quick one second burst of airsoft lubricant down the barrel of your gun every couple of thousand rounds will help keep BBs moving smoothly through the barrel. Let the lubricant sit for a few minute and then fire a few rounds to help blow the excess oil out of the barrel. If your gun has "hop-up", this procedure will also help lube the hop-up mechanism.

External hinges or other moving parts should be cleaned regularly with a small brush (like a toothbrush) to loosen any dirt particles or other debris. Then blow or wipe the debris away, spray a little silicon lubricant on a small clean rag and wipe down the hinges, springs, or other moving parts. Finally, use another dry cloth to wipe off any excess oil.

Lubricating the gearbox on an AEG every 25,000 to 30,000 shots can also help prolong the life of your AEG. However, to do this you have to disassemble the gun including the gearbox. That can be a complicated and difficult job -- if you want to lube the gearbox but aren't comfortable disassembling your gun, try taking it to a local airsoft dealer for maintenance.

Is it OK to reuse BBs?
The short answer is "NO", do not reuse BBs. When you fire a BB it's liable to get scratched, dirty or slightly dented. Reusing a damaged BB (even one that only has a minor defect) can cause the BB to bang around as it's traveling down the barrel of your gun and wind up damaging the inside of the barrel. If you've simply fired a BB into a gel foam target it may be perfectly OK, but airsoft BBs are so inexpensive (except for the really high-end ones) -- why take a chance on something happening to your much more expensive airsoft gun?

What are the best airsoft BBs?
There are a number of good brands of BBs: Excel, MadBull, TSD, Matrix and G&G among others. What's best for you depends on what type of airsoft gun you have. Generally the more expensive AEGs and sniper rifles do best with the slightly heavier BBs (.25 grams and up). The heavier the BB the less it's going to be affected by wind or other factors and the straighter it's going to fly. No matter what type of gun you have or what weight you choose, always buy a reputable brand and look for BBs that are seamless and highly polished.

Are there any special types of airsoft BBs?
There are several special varieties of airsoft BBs. A number of companies produce biodegradable BBs, made with a type of plastic that eventually breaks down and disintegrates. Tracer or "glow-in-the-dark" BBs put off a visible light when they're fired so they can be easily tracked, making them popular for use at night. And there are also "marker" BBs, a relative newcomer to the market. Marker BBs have a very light powder coating and leave a visible mark where they hit -- making it easier to tell if a particular player in an airsoft contest has been

"shot".

Should I use biodegradable BBs for outdoor shooting?
Biodegradable BBs sound great, but they have several drawbacks. First and most important, it takes years for a "biodegradable" BB to, well, biodegrade. And they can be poisonous to birds. The quality of these BBs is also somewhat uneven, with some having visible seams or defects -- and they tend to be less accurate. However, due to the potential damage regular BBs can do to the environment, manufacturers are working to produce better and more reliable bio BBs. As the quality improves biodegradable BBs will probably take over a larger share of the market. Environmental concerns may also cause an increase in indoor gaming where used BBs can be collected and disposed of properly.

What is a "Hi-Cap" magazine?
Hi-Cap is an abbreviation for High-Capacity. Hi-cap magazines for AEGs can often hold as much as ten times as many BBs as a normal magazine. The obvious advantage to using one is that it cuts way down on time spent reloading. Hi-cap magazines use a special coiled band spring that's much more space-efficient than the standard springs. All you have to remember is that a hi-cap magazine in an AEG won't work unless there's enough tension on the spring. Every so often you have to wind the wheel on the bottom of the magazine to move BBs from the holding chamber to the feed chute; when you hear a click you know the chute is full and the spring is fully compressed. Also, it's a good idea to keep a funnel handy to help load the BBs into a hi-cap. When you store your gun, remember to release the tension on the magazine spring by emptying the BBs; that will help extend the life of the magazine considerably. One other thing to keep in mind with hi-cap magazines is that they can make a rattling noise when you move due to the loose BBs in the holding chamber.

NOTE: Hi-Cap magazines are not allowed on some fields (particularly in milsim games), since they aren't realistic -- real firearms don't have that kind of ammo capacity.

What are "low cap" and "mid cap" magazines?

Some airsoft players use low capacity magazines (100 BBs or less) in their AEGs to more closely simulate real world weapons. Mid-cap magazines have been slightly modified to hold additional rounds (usually between 100 and 200 BBs).

What are "classic" airsoft guns?
The term "classic guns" is normally used in airsoft to refer to early-model gas guns from the 1990s which were powered by a liquid propellant (R-12, also marketed as Freon-12). Classic guns have been replaced by AEGs, CO_2 and propane powered airsoft guns.

What's the most expensive airsoft gun?
Just taking a quick survey, the most expensive one I could come up with at the moment is a Systema PTW (Professional Training Weapon) that fires at 460 feet per second, that features a custom adjustable stock and grips and a 12" stainless steel outer barrel. This particular model goes for around $4300 -- and there may well be even more expensive guns out there somewhere.

Which type of airsoft gun works best in cold weather?
Spring powered pistols and rifles are largely unaffected by temperature and will operate about as well in cold weather as in warm weather. Gas guns (both CO_2 and propane or green gas guns) perform worse in colder weather due to a drop in gas pressure with temperature. In fact, in frigid temperatures gas guns may not operate at all. Electric guns are also affected by cold, but generally not as much as a CO_2 or gas gun. One thing to keep in mind is that rapid firing also causes a temperature drop in your CO_2 or propane supply - if you're outside in winter it helps to pause slightly between shots to reduce this additional cooling effect.

What is a "ghillie" suit?
Some airsofters who play the role of sniper dress in ghillie suits for added realism. A ghillie suit covers the whole body and is designed to camouflage the wearer. It's usually made of net or cloth and covered with strips of cloth or twine that can be used to attach twigs and leaves. The overall effect is designed to conceal the wearer by making him look like part of the

surrounding foliage.

What is a "DMR"?
A DMR (Designated Marksman Rifle) is a rifle designed for longer range accuracy than a standard infantry rifle, but usually not as specialized as a sniper's rifle.

What's a "PDW"?
A Personal Defense Weapon (PDW) is a compact semi-automatic or full automatic weapon similar to a submachine gun. PDWs have advantages and disadvantages over submachine guns. PDWs fire an armor-piercing round which gives them better range and hitting power, but they also use a special cartridge size which isn't compatible with other rifles and pistols. PDWs never really caught on with the military in general, but they are used by some Special Forces units. Current models of PDWs include the FN P90, the Heckler & Koch MP7, and the Magpul PDR (a bullpup style PDW).

What does "MOLLE" stand for?
MOLLE (pronounced "Molly") is an acronym for MOdular Lightweight Load-carrying Equipment. It's a system used by the U.S. Army for attaching packs and equipment. A soldier's vest has rows of heavy duty nylon stitched onto the vest, and those nylon straps are used to attach MOLLE compatible items for the soldier to carry.

What parts of an AEG can be upgraded?
Here's a quick list of some parts of your AEG that can be upgraded:

1) Battery (a higher voltage produces a higher rate of fire and the higher the Milliamp-Hour rating (mAH), the more BBs you can fire per charge - but do some research to make sure a given battery isn't too powerful for your AEG).
2) Motor (as with batteries, make sure your gun can handle a given motor; too powerful a motor will strip the gears on your AEG).

3) Gears (replacing the standard gears in your AEG - the sector, bevel, and spur gears - with metal gears can extend the

life of your AEG and also allow you to upgrade to a more powerful spring or motor).

4) Bushings (bushings are what the gears rotate on and replacing plastic bushings with metal ones can help keep the bushings from breaking).

5) Barrels (tighter barrels can increase muzzle velocity)

6) Spring (a stronger spring forces the piston forward faster, but you will probably need to upgrade other parts of your AEG to handle the increased spring strength).

7) Piston (the piston is wound back by the motor, then slammed forward by the spring; metal pistons provide more durability but can damage your gears if fired in full automatic mode).

How do you adjust the hop-up on an airsoft gun?
Find a place where you can fire a few rounds without disturbing anyone, with as little wind as possible (and be sure to use the same BBs you intend to use in a game). Set up a target about the same distance away as you will most likely be using it in an airsoft game (usually 40 to 50 feet). Brace your gun on a chair or some other object so that the gun won't move around, center your front sight on the bullseye and squeeze off several shots. If the BBs missed the bullseye in a random fashion (some low, some high), start over with a fresh target and try again. If the BBs are all too high, you need to turn the hop-up down and vice-versa.

The rear sight on my gun can be adjusted up or down. Why?
If your gun has no hop-up adjustment you need to be able to move the rear sight up or down to zero your gun for the range you want. Fire a few shots (while steadying your gun on something to minimize movement) and see where the shots land. If they are too high move the rear sight downward - and vice versa.

How do I adjust my sights if my shots are going to the

right or left?

Assuming your rear sight can be adjusted to one side or the other, if your shots are left of target move the rear sight to the right; if your shots are right of target move the rear sight to the left.

Airsoft Games

What's the minimum number of people you need for an airsoft game?

A reasonable number might be six players for a two-team game. For a more complicated game scenario you would probably want at least twelve people, while full-scale milsim games work best with large numbers, say 50 or more players.

Can an airsoft match be played indoors?

Yes, considering the low-impact of airsoft BBs and their tendency to shatter rather than bounce off of metal objects, airsoft games are often held indoors. There are a lot of businesses that have sprung up that offer indoor facilities for airsoft competitions. A good many of these places include realistic tactical setups such as mock-ups of buildings, trucks, etc.

How do I find a place to play airsoft?

Ask at a local airsoft store if you have one nearby or check airsoft forums for playing areas near you. If there's a paintball complex close to you check there too - some paintball facilities have added airsoft playing areas.

What are some websites with good airsoft forums?

www.airsoftohio.com, www.airsoftgiforum.com, www.airsoftforum.com, www.airsoftsociety.com, www.airsoftretreat.com, www.arniesairsoft.co.uk, www.airsoftcore.com – and there are many other good sites if you do a little searching.

Are airsoft playing fields insured?

Insurance may not be a necessity for a few friends playing on private property, but any airsoft field available for public use should definitely have property, liability and medical insurance coverage.

Before you start gaming at a new field check to make sure what coverage they have; if they have a website you may be able to find out there - otherwise ask the field operator. If you decide to open a field yourself, the insurance company will probably require a copy of the lease agreement (if you're leasing the property), field rules and regulations, and a legal waiver form of some sort for players to sign.

Do airsoft playing fields have rules?
Almost all airsoft fields (areas specially set up for airsoft games) have specific rules. Outdoor fields usually limit airsoft guns to those with a muzzle velocity of around 350 feet per second or less. Indoor facilities often have even lower fps limits. This rule is usually enforced by chronographing each player's gun before a match to make sure the weapons meet the muzzle velocity limits.

In addition all players are required to have eye protection (either goggles or face masks) and outdoor fields may want players to use biodegradable BBs only.

Are there different types of airsoft games?
Airsoft games fall pretty much into one of two categories: CQB or "Close Quarters Battle" games, which are normally played indoors and "Woodland" games, which are normally played outdoors. CQB games are also sometimes referred to as MOUT (Military Operations on Urban Terrain) or CQC (Close Quarters Combat) games and center around building-clearing scenarios. Woodland games are usually played over large wooded areas and tend to be longer and more involved than CQB.

What exactly is CQB?
CQB or Close Quarters Battle is a combat game played within a small area (usually in an urban setting) where the emphasis is on fast movement and firepower. Quite often one team takes the part of an occupying force which has fortified itself in a group of buildings and the other team attempts to root them out and capture the "town". Proper planning and communication between teammates can be vital in winning or losing a CQB game. Some factors to remember: stay low, move fast, keep your gun up and in front of you, and walk quickly rather than running -- running makes more noise. Also, assign specific areas to members of your fire team that they are supposed to cover; front, flanks, and rear.

What's a typical airsoft game look like?
Here's a link to a YouTube video showing a typical CQB (Close
Quarters Battle) game: http://www.youtube.com/watch?
v=xNjgL0YDMCw .

What are some airsoft game drills I can do?
Since you're very unlikely to damage yourself with an airsoft
gun, there are a lot of techniques you can practice safely. You
might include drills such as shooting, changing magazines on
the fly and resuming shooting, hitting hanging targets or small,
fast-moving targets, or shooting at multiple randomly-placed
targets. You can also work on various shooting positions --
standing, kneeling, prone, or moving in various directions
relative to the target.

How many BBs should I bring when I go to an airsoft game?
For informal neighborhood games a few hundred to a thousand
BBs should be OK. For a typical all-day game at an airsoft
field, you should probably bring three to four thousand BBs.

Do I need to bring an extra battery for my AEG when I go to a game?
If you're going to be playing in cold weather (cold weather
drains batteries faster) or if you're going to be playing all day,
you should bring an extra fully charged battery just to be safe.
And if you happen to have an extra AEG or other primary
weapon it's always good to bring a spare gun in case your AEG
conks out while you're playing.

Do airsoft fields let you climb trees?
Assuming the field you play on has trees, it can be tempting to
get a better look at the playing field but the answer is generally
"No". The tactical benefits are outweighed by the risk of injury.
Plus there's nothing quite like getting stranded in a tree when
your team falls back and becoming target practice for the other
side.

What's a "load-out"?
"Load-out" refers to the weapons and airsoft gear each player
in an airsoft game carries. A player's load-out will normally

depend on what role he or she has on the team - rifleman, support gunner, sniper, or scout.

Is it OK to play an airsoft game in the rain?
Yes, unless there's severe weather or lightning around. Rain does change the game somewhat; goggles tend to fog up more and it becomes harder to detect movement. Also, if it's raining fairly heavily BBs can actually be deflected by the raindrops, which minimize the distance at which you can make a "kill".

Will it damage my AEG to play an airsoft game in the rain?
Unless you have a really cheap AEG rain (short of a torrential downpour) shouldn't be a problem. Just try not to get water in the barrel or completely submerge your AEG. Some players wrap a trash bag or something similar around their AEGs, but that's really not necessary. After the game is over though, be sure to disconnect your battery, dry your gun out thoroughly, and apply silicon spray in the normal places.

Are radios used in airsoft matches and if so, what kind?
In larger airsoft games radios are often used to communicate between teams and team members. Radios used in airsoft normally fall into one of two categories: PMR (Personal Mobile Radio) or FRS (Family Radio Service). PMR and FRS radios are reasonably priced and tend to be small and compact with short antennas. They are low powered, can operate on FM channels and don't require a license to operate. Keep in mind though that because they are low-power radios they don't work well for penetrating through dense woods or over long distances.

What is "leapfrogging"?
Leapfrogging (also referred to as a "bounding overwatch") is one of the most basic infantry tactics. An attacking force divides into two parts (each of which may consist of a team or just individual soldiers). Team A for example provides covering fire for Team B while Team B advances a short distance toward the enemy; then Team B takes cover and provides covering fire for Team A while Team A advances a short distance past Team A's position. Then the sequence is repeated until the enemy position is taken.

What is "overwatch"?
Overwatch is a tactic where one unit stays stationary and provides covering fire for an advancing unit. The overwatch unit has to taken a position where it can observe the terrain ahead and concentrate effective fire on any enemy positions.

What is "camping"?
Camping is staying in one position for a long period of time. Players (other than snipers) should normally keep moving, working toward an objective or hunting opposition players. If you have a large number of players camping out just waiting to shoot someone who happens by, it tends to ruin the flow of the game.

What is "grazing fire"?
Grazing fire is a horizontal line of fire (usually 3 or 4 feet off the ground) laid down by machineguns. Normally grazing fire is used when an enemy force is attacking your position.

Can you handcuff an opposing player or tie him up?
Generally, airsoft fields don't allow you to physically restrain a player; you simply touch the player and tell him he's restrained. To what extent the player is restrained depends on the rules for the particular game you're playing. For example it may be that only his hands are considered to be tied and he can still run away.

If your gun is hit by a BB does that count as a "kill"?
It depends on the rules for the particular game you're playing. In some cases a gun hit is a kill, in some cases your gun is considered "broken" and (at least temporarily) unusable, and in some games a gun hit is simply ignored (although players may call out "gun hit" just to acknowledge the hit). In games where your weapon is hit and considered broken you may be forced to use a backup weapon for the rest of the game or there may be special rules about "repairing" your gun.

Are there any "non-lethal" hits in airsoft?
Depending on the game rules, sometimes games are played where a hit on a leg or arm isn't considered a "kill". Under those types of rules, a hit in the leg may mean that you can't

walk (but can still crawl) and a hit in the arm means you can't use that arm any more. Also, if you're wearing body armor the rules may specify that you have to hit there a certain number of times before you're "dead".

What about searching another player for weapons or important papers?

Maps, plans, weapons or whatever should be kept in outside pockets where they are easily visible and quickly found if a player is "searched".

Is it OK to wait just outside of the other team's respawn area?

Occasionally a player or players will decide to "camp" just outside of the other team's respawn area and shoot that team's players as they reenter the game. On most fields that's considered cheating and in fact, opposing players usually have to stay a certain minimum distance away from the other team's respawn area.

Can you take part in an airsoft game without being on either side?

On occasion there are games that make use of "civilians" or "natives". Adding non-combatants to a game can actually make the game both more realistic and more complex. For example you may have a scenario where your team needs to obtain information from the native populace, but you don't know which of them are enemy sympathizers and which are "friendlies".

What kind of sights do I need for airsoft games?

Unless you're a sniper you can probably do alright with just iron sights (assuming that's what came on your gun) or by practicing "instinct shooting" (shooting without aiming). Snipers or any other long distance shooters will probably have a telescopic sight of some kind. A lot of other players use a "red dot" sight because they feel it gives them better accuracy and conserves BBs compared to instinct shooting. Unless your gun is pretty well zeroed in and you can hit your target with the first or second shot, instinct shooting can chew up your supply of BBs as you "walk" the stream of BBs onto your target. If you're into strict realism, most combat troops only have iron sights on their rifle and are trained to use them if there's time. However, if an enemy soldier pops up right in front of them, they're also trained to shoot simply by pointing the barrel at the other guy's center of mass (chest area) and pulling the trigger.

NOTE: "instinct shooting" is basically the same as "point shooting", "quick kill", or "quick fire" systems, all of which are based on the idea that (with practice) your weapon will fire whereever your eyes are focused. Keep in mind that any shooting of this kind is intended mainly for close-up targets.

Can you use tear gas in an airsoft game?
If your field allows it you can use simulated mace or tear gas (by using a spray bottle or something similar) and any player hit by it has to react according to the rules of the game.

Are "marker" BBs better than regular BBs for airsoft games?
In a normal airsoft game everyone is pretty much on the honor system; that is, you are expected to call out if you feel a BB hit you and acknowledge that you've been "shot". Of course that approach can create a lot of arguments, especially if a player is hit by a BB shot from long range and doesn't feel it or realize he's been hit. Marker BBs are intended (at least partially) to help solve that problem by leaving a visible mark when they hit. However, they oftentimes leave only a very faint mark, especially in cold weather. Plus there's the problem of whether a particular mark is new or the residue from a previous hit. All in all, marker BBs may be useful in some scenarios but their use is very limited right now.

How are "medics" used in an airsoft game?
Using medics introduces a new dimension to the game. Medics can heal wounded players or respawn dead ones. There are a lot of variations to this idea though -- do you have just one medic or more than one, can a medic heal someone instantly or does it take a certain amount of time, can a medic heal himself, and so on.

What is a "support" gunner?

Support gunners are an important of an airsoft team. They provide rapid, high volume fire support for the team in both offensive and defensive situation. Generally, a player designated as a support gunner will use an airsoft gun similar to the Army's M-249 SAW (Squad Automatic Weapon), which can lay down continuous heavy fire. The most important duty of the support gunner is to provide suppressing fire, to try to force the "enemy" players to keep their heads down while the other members of the team move forward or fall back.

Do I need a tactical vest?
The main purpose of a tactical vest is storage - storage for extra magazines, BBs, a speedloader and other items. If you're taking part in a game that's going to last a couple of hours or longer, a vest can be very useful. Look for one that's durable but lightweight, comfortable and has plenty of storage pockets. Also, check the zippers and Velcro closures carefully to make sure they work easily and close securely. There's a wide range in prices for tactical vests, but you should be able to find a decent one for less than fifty dollars.

What's a good way to train to play airsoft?
First of all, practice target shooting with each of your weapons - being able to hit your opponents during game play is the single most important skill to practice. Another good way to train if you're going to play "woodland" airsoft is to take long hikes and/or bike rides wearing full airsoft gear (or at least a fairly heavy backpack) - that really helps to build physical stamina. Playing SWAT or military simulation computer games can give you an idea of what most airsoft matches are like and what kind of strategy and tactics you may see in a real game.

What is "blowback"?
In a gas airsoft gun, "blowback" refers to cycling the slide or bolt to simulate a real firearm's operation. As each BB is fired some of the gas is used to force the slide or bolt backwards momentarily. As the gas escapes the slide or bolt moves forward again, automatically chambering the next BB, just the way it would in an actual firearm. There are also electric blowback guns (EBBs) which operate the same way, using power from the gun's battery pack rather than gas pressure.

What is a "respawn point"?

Most airsoft games allow a player who has been shot and "killed" to get back into the game by moving to some area designated as a "respawn point" and waiting a certain length of time. Eventually the player is considered to have been brought back to life and can go back into the field of play.

What is a "death" or "dead" rag?

In some airsoft games, players who have been "shot" are required to wear a certain type of rag while they're moving to the "respawn" point to be reborn and reenter the game. The rag signifies that the person is a "dead man walking" and isn't an active player at that point. At times a "dead" player moving through the field of play may also call out "Dead man walking" to alert others that he or she is a non-combatant.

Should I call out when I hit somebody with a BB?

Calling out your hits is discouraged in most airsoft games. Airsoft games operate on the honor system and depend on players acknowledging on their own when they've been hit.

Does a single hit always count as a "kill"?

It depends on the rules you're using (there are very few hard and fast rules in airsoft). One variation is a game where the first hit knocks you to the ground and leaves you "bleeding", with a second hit being a kill shot. If a medic can get to you within a certain length of time you can be healed on the spot, but even while you're on the ground "bleeding out" you can still fire your weapon until you finally "die".

What if I'm hit by a BB fired by a teammate?
If you're hit by friendly fire it still counts as a "kill" shot; raise your hands/weapon, shout "hit!" and head for the respawn point.

Is there a minimum age for playing at an airsoft field?

At most fields there is a minimum age (anywhere from 10 to 18) in order to play - and anyone under the age of 18 has to have a parent or guardian sign a waiver allowing them to play.

I've heard there are metal airsoft BBs - can I use them in a game?
There are 6mm metal BBs for use in airsoft guns but they are not allowed on any legitimate airsoft field. Metal BBs are for target practice only - they are too dangerous for game play (and over time they will damage the barrel of an airsoft gun).

What are "safe areas"?
Some games allow for a "safe" area for each team - a place where team members can go to rest, reload, and replenish supplies. Teams may also regroup at their safe area to plan their next operation.

What are "barrel bags" and "barrel blockers"?
Airsoft fields generally require that anyone not actively playing has to cover the barrel of his or her weapon with a bag or with a device that fits over the end of the barrel. Usually the gun's safety is also required to be on, with the magazine removed.

What happens if a non-player enters the field of an airsoft game?
If a bystander or passer-by turns up in the field of play, all players are required to immediately call out something like "Cease fire, Blind Man" and stop shooting until the field is cleared.

Are knives ever allowed in airsoft games?
Obviously real knives aren't allowed - however some fields permit the use of rubber or plastic training knives and kills can be made by touching an opponent with the knife or by throwing the knife and hitting another player. Even if training knives aren't allowed, some provision is usually made for simulating a "knife kill" by simply touching an opponent. The main reason for allowing so-called knife kills is to avoid situations where one player has to shoot another at point-blank range. If you shoot someone who's that close you could actually break the skin if the BB hits an exposed part of the body. Alternatively, players may be permitted to make "courtesy kills" at close range by forcing an opponent to "surrender".
How do you acknowledge being hit in an airsoft game at night?

At night, when you can't see a person raise his or her hand, mini-flashlights or glow sticks are sometimes used by players to show that they have been shot.

In an airsoft game how do you know a player has been hit?

Airsoft games basically rely on the honor system in determining hits. Each player is expected to acknowledge being hit by raising a hand and yelling out something like "I've been hit". Of course there are instances when a player may not feel a BB hit, especially if the BB came from a sniper or other player a long distance away. Or a player may simply feel like the BB actually missed him. So how do you resolve problems like this? The general feeling among airsoft players seems to be to rely on the honor system combined with a sense of fair play (rather than trying options like marker BBs). After all, airsoft games aren't really a matter of life and death -- the object is simply to have fun and enjoy the game.

What are the limits on muzzle velocity for airsoft gaming?

In the U.S., limits vary over a wide range although for most airsoft facilities they are usually somewhere around 330 feet per second up to about 400 feet per second. There may also different limits for different types of weapons (AEGs, sniper rifles, etc.). Currently, the United Kingdom, Ireland and Italy impose a energy limit of one joule (100 meters per second or roughly 330 feet per second) when using .2 gram BBs. Other countries (those that impose limits) generally fall within the same range.

Do airsoft goggles or glasses have to meet a certain standard?

Many airsoft teams and playing fields require goggles that seal completely around the eye. In addition, goggles and shooting glasses may also be required to meet the ANSI Z87.1-2003 standard for eye protection (that standard being the ability to withstand 3 joules of impact energy).

How long do airsoft matches last?

Large scale milsim (military simulation) games can last for

several days, but most airsoft matches are over in a few hours or a day at most. Also, an airsoft event is usually broken down into a number of separate scenarios or games (capture the flag, hostage rescue, etc.), so you may end up competing in just some of the games. Of course informal neighborhood skirmishes may go for 30 minutes or from dawn to dusk (or later) depending on the enthusiasm and endurance of the players.

Does everyone compete as part of a team?

Just as in real life combat, everyone has to depend on other members of the team in order to succeed. If you enjoy working on your own though, your best bet is to try to gain a spot on a team as a sniper. The goal of a sniper is to locate a good firing position, find cover and try to stay invisible and that's usually a one man job (or at most two men - a sniper and his spotter).

What do I need if I want to be a sniper?

One primary thing you'll need is patience. Snipers often have to lie quietly in wait for some time before they get a chance to take down an opposing player. You will also need a good sniper rifle and those are somewhat expensive. Make sure you get a rifle with a muzzle velocity of at least 350 fps since you're going to firing at targets some distance away. You may also want to see about modifying your weapon to add another 50 fps or so (be aware that for rifles in the 400 fps range you'll probably want to use .28 gram or heavier BBs). And finally, a note of caution - sniper rifles don't work well for skirmishing; make sure you really want to play the role of sniper or you may end up having to buy a regular AEG for skirmishing in addition to your sniper rifle.

Are all airsoft games military scenarios?

No, many airsoft matches are designed around other situations such as a police drug bust, federal agents taking down a group of terrorists, or starship troopers fighting alien invaders. The basic framework of an airsoft game can be modified in all kinds of ways depending on what kind of situation the players want to recreate.

If I'm "killed" do I have to return to the respawn point?

Players will sometimes wait the required time to respawn

before returning to the game, but won't bother to go all the way back to the respawn point. This is usually considered a form of cheating, because it allows you to reenter the game quicker and possibly closer to the action than if you made your way to and from the respawn point.

What is "dead shooting"?
"Dead shooting" occurs when a player is in a firefight and gets hit but fires a last burst at an opponent as he's "dying".

What are some examples of airsoft game scenarios?
Here are a few suggestions:
1) Rescue prisoners from a POW camp
2) Recreate an historic battle
3) Take down a group of terrorists or drug lords
4) Capture the flag
5) Attack a fortified enemy position
6) Two rival urban gangs fighting for the same turf
7) Starship troopers fighting alien invaders
8) Police versus gangsters
9) Recover certain items placed at random locations

What is an "SOI" card?
A SOI (Signal Operating Instructions) card contains instructions regarding radio call signs and code words, as well as visual and verbal signals to be used in communicating between individuals or fire teams.

What's the difference between "cover" and "concealment"?
Concealment helps hide you and makes it difficult for the enemy to see you. Cover not only helps hide you, it provides a barrier that the enemy can't shoot through.

What are some of the special roles for airsoft team members?
In addition to the standard members of an airsoft team, there are some special roles that can be added to bring additional elements into the game. Probably the most popular role is that of the sniper, a player who basically works by himself (or with a partner who handles security for the sniper). Snipers, by

striking from concealment, provide a surprise long-range threat for enemy forces.

Grenadiers offer another interesting addition to a team, providing extra firepower and a larger killzone than small arms fire. A grenadier can also be useful in attacking fortified positions.
Heavy weapons team members using a SAW (Squad Automatic Weapon) or something similar can give effective covering fire for the team, forcing your opponents to keep their heads down.

Adding medics to the game also opens up new possibilities, depending on what rules you adopt as to how and when a medic can "heal" team members who have been "shot".

One other role that's sometimes included in airsoft games is the "Engineer". Although an Engineer is usually associated with deploying Claymores or other types of mines, this role can lend itself to some interesting modifications. One example might be adding obstacles to the field that require a team to wait a certain length of time to cross unless they have an Engineer.

What is a "recon" player's job in an airsoft game?
Recon (reconnaissance) players are the intelligence gatherers for an airsoft team. Their job is to sneak in behind enemy lines and learn as much as they can about the terrain, the opposing team and their equipment, obstacles, booby traps, enemy command points, and anything else of importance. Recon members travel light and avoid contact with the opposing team if at all possible. Their purpose is to gather and pass on as much information as they can without engaging the enemy.

What's a "tactical carry"?
There are several standard ways to carry your rifle when you're moving in a combat area. With a tactical carry, assuming you are right-handed, you carry the rifle pointed upward at roughly 45 degrees with the butt stock next to your body at about hip level and the muzzle in front of your eyes at eye level.

What's the "alert carry"?
The alert carry is somewhat the opposite of the tactical carry, in

that the rifle is pointed down, with the butt stock against your shoulder and your rifle at about a 45 degree downward angle. This is also known as a "Low Ready" position.

What's the "ready position"?
When you're expecting contact with the enemy at any moment, you normally carry your rifle in the "ready" position, pointed straight out in front of you just below eye level. This is also referred to as a "High Ready" position.

What's the "retention position"?
If you're not expecting immediate contact with the enemy, you can carry your rifle comfortably by pulling it back against your abdomen and carrying it tilted up at about a 45 degree angle.

What's the maximum effective range of an AEG?
For most standard (unmodified) AEGs, the maximum effective range is somewhere around 100 to 150 feet (30 to 45 meters).

What's the best way to reload if you're under fire?
Leave the safety off but move your finger off the trigger. Press the magazine release button with your non-firing hand, catch the empty magazine with your firing hand and secure it somewhere. Then grab the loaded magazine with your firing hand, insert it into the AEG and, once the mag is fully inserted and locked, grab the pistol grip again and get your finger back on the trigger.

When should I use full automatic firing mode?
Firing on full automatic is almost always less accurate than semi-automatic because your point of aim tends to drift as you're holding the trigger down. In general, you should use full auto if you're engaging multiple targets that are bunched together and are at close range; use semi-automatic mode if you're engaging a single target or multiple targets that are spread out and farther away. Even if you're using a hi-cap magazine that holds several hundred BBS, you can empty the magazine in 15 seconds or less if you're firing on full auto. Also, full automatic creates a stream of BBs that can give away your location much faster than short bursts of BBs.

When you do use full auto mode, make sure you have a firm grip on your rifle and hold it as tightly as possible against your body to help steady your aim. If possible, fire from a prone or supported position.

What is "tracking" and "trapping"?

When you're firing at a moving target, "tracking" is moving your weapon and point of aim along with the target. "Trapping" is picking out a point ahead of the target and firing as the target reaches that point.

What is "quick fire"?

Quick fire is just what it sounds like -- firing "from the hip" in a situation where you don't have time to actually aim your rifle.

What's the difference between a "clip" and a "magazine"?

A magazine is a container that ammunition is loaded into, while a clip is a device (normally a metal strip) that holds multiple rounds of ammunition together so they can be loaded into a magazine as a unit rather than inserted individually. For airsoft guns, you're always dealing with magazines, not clips.

What about taking an airsoft gun out in public?

If you're transporting an airsoft gun (say from your house to an airsoft field), make sure your gun is unloaded and that the orange tip is in place, and put the gun in a securely fastened case or container.

What's a "woodland" airsoft game?

Airsoft games played indoors are usually referred to as "urban" games, while games played outdoors are referred to as "woodland" games.

Is a longer barrel always better than a shorter one?

There's a point (somewhere around 15 to 16 inches) where a longer barrel actually decreases performance. If the barrel is too long, a vacuum effect can form behind the BB as it's traveling through the barrel and act to slow it down.

If you're near the enemy, how can you communicate

with your team?

If you're too close to talk to each other (or to use radios even if you have them), then you need to have a system of hand signals. There are some fairly standard hand signals, such as holding up an open hand to tell the team members to halt or holding up a clinched fist to tell them to "freeze". Other signals that should be worked out ahead of time might include "move up", "get down", "take cover", "fan out", "pull back", and so forth. Try to make the signals as meaningful as possible -- for example, a downward motion with an open hand to signal "get down" or pointing backward to signal "pull back".

One possible exception to this might be if you want to try to confuse the enemy by shouting out bogus orders or calls for help, etc. For example, you might have your teammates spread out in an ambush and suddenly yell out an order to "fall back", hoping to get the other side to rush forward into the ambush.

What if you have to retreat?

Try to handle a retreat in a backward leapfrog fashion. That is, have some of your team take cover and provide covering fire while other team members pull back and find cover. Then the members of the team that have been providing covering fire fall back while the rest of the team covers them and the cycle starts over again.

What's a "linear" ambush?

To prepare a linear ambush you position your team in a line alongside the opposing force's line of advance and take cover. Normally you divide your team into three groups, with a "blocking" group on the left of your main force and another blocking group on the right. Once the enemy begins to pass directly in front of your main force or "kill" group, you open fire; the blocking groups on your flanks keep the enemy troops from retreating or advancing, closing the "kill box". You may also have a "security" group, whose job is to provide covering fire for the rest of your team as you pull back from the ambush site.

What's an "L-shaped" ambush?

An L-shaped ambush is virtually the same as the linear ambush except that one of your flanking (or "blocking") groups is moved into the line of advance of the opposing troops.

What's a "defensive" ambush?
If you're retreating under fire, one tactic is to try to gain a little separation and set up an ambush for your pursuers. Position your team members in a sort of inverted triangle with the base of the triangle toward the enemy troops and your best marksman at the apex of the triangle. Have everyone take cover and wait for the enemy troops to enter the triangle. As soon as they do, have your marksman open fire first; then have the other team members join in, forming a "kill box" of sorts and hopefully forcing the enemy to pull back.

What about camouflage for your face?
For woodland (outdoors) games, you may want to paint or otherwise camouflage your face to make yourself harder to see. Camo sticks are inexpensive, easy to find online and you can get them in various combinations of light green, dark green, and sand. Use dark colors on the shiny areas of your face and lighter colors on the darker areas (such as under your eyes and nose and under your chin). Don't forget your eyelids; and you can also apply some paint to your neck, arms and hands. Use an irregular pattern and, in wooded areas, add come dark vertical lines to fit in with the surrounding vegetation.

What about camouflage for your helmet or hat?
If you're playing in a wooded area you may want to attach some leaves or grass to your helmet or hat. Even some dirt or mud smeared on a helmet can help make it harder to spot.

When do you use binoculars or a monocular in an airsoft game?
Traditionally binoculars or monoculars are used by a spotter working with a sniper to help pick out targets at a distance. There's another situation where they can useful though, even at short distances. If you're in bright light looking into dark foliage, binoculars and monoculars are light gathering devices - looking through one gives you a brighter picture of the area you're watching, which can help you spot detail you wouldn't see with the naked eye.

Who are "airsoft marshals"?

Most airsoft fields or facilities have "marshals" who supervise game play. You should always make it a point to listen to the marshals and do what they say - they're there to make sure no one gets hurt, that the game is played fairly and within the rules, and that everyone has a good time.

Can I try airsoft gaming without having to spend a lot of money?

Many airsoft gaming facilities rent weapons, safety equipment, and other airsoft gear. That way you can give airsofting a try with a minimum of expense and if you don't like it you haven't wasted your money.

Is there a difference between a "gun" and a "rifle"?

Technically, a "gun" is a firearm where the inside of the barrel is smooth; a rifle has grooves (or "rifling") cut into the inside of the barrel to help guide the bullet, keep it from touching the barrel, and give it greater range and stability. In the military the term "guns" applies mainly to artillery pieces - almost all real steel pistols and rifles have rifled barrels. The barrels of most airsoft weapons however are not rifled, so they are "guns" in the truest sense. Hop-up devices take the place of rifling in airsoft guns and perform the same function by preventing the BB from hitting the inside of the barrel, stabilizing it's flight and giving it greater range.

I'm on a tight budget - what brand of AEG should I look at?

Your best bet may be a Jing Gong gun; they're relatively inexpensive, come with a battery and charger, and perform as well as many higher priced guns.

Can I shoot someone during a game who's only a couple of feet away?

Many airsoft fields or facilities have a MED or minimum engagement distance (usually around 20 feet). You have to be at least that far away to shoot at another player. Snipers (who usually have higher-powered rifles) are required to be even farther away. If you're within the minimum distance from an opponent and can't shoot him, you can try to force him to surrender or (in some games) you can make a "safety" kill just by tapping his shoulder.

NOTE: Minimum engagement rules vary considerably. Some fields (especially CQB fields) may not have a minimum distance of any kind. At other facilities there may be a one minimum for snipers, a different one for AEGs, and a third one for sidearms (and there even be different distances for different types of sidearms).

What is "blind shooting"?
"Blind shooting" is firing without actually being able to see your target. Airsoft fields often have a rule against shooting unless you can see the other player or players; for example, firing blindly around a corner you could wind up firing right at someone's face at point blank range. There are exceptions though - for example, if you're in a woodland game and you can tell that opposing players are concealed in a certain area but can't get a clear look at them, you may fire into that area in order to try and flush them out.

What's a "stock weld"?
A stock weld is the point of contact between your cheek and the stock of your weapon. Assuming that you're using the sights on your gun and not "firing from the hip", it's a good idea to make sure you've got your cheek pressed firmly against the stock. If you ever fire a high-powered rifle you'll need to use a good stock weld or else the recoil can slam the stock right into your face. Just ask trainees in Basic Training who didn't follow their Drill Sergeant's advice - you'll find a lot of badly bruised cheeks.

What does "slicing the pie" mean?
Sometime you'll hear this expression, usually in connection with room clearing in CQB. Basically it means that as you approach a corner or doorway, move ahead slowly until you can see a small section or "slice" of what's in the room or around the corner. Check everything within your field of vision for clues as to what may be waiting for you, then move ahead a little farther and check the next "slice".

What is "trigger squeeze" and why is it important?

One of the most common reasons for missing the target when you shoot is flinching or jerking your finger on the trigger. The term "trigger squeeze" refers to proper technique in pulling the trigger - pulling straight back with a steady pressure. Flinching (because you're anticipating the weapon's recoil) is not usually that big a problem in airsoft, since very few airsoft guns have significant recoil. The most common problem, jerking the trigger, is usually caused by trying to rush the shot - pulling the trigger as quickly as possible once you've got the target in your sights. You want to shoot quickly but without doing anything to move the gun's point of aim as you fire. Also, keep in mind that trying to keep an extremely tight grip on the weapon to prevent it from moving usually results in over-compensating and pulling the barrel off-line in the opposite direction from jerking or flinching. For best results, just hold the gun firmly, stay calm, and use a steady pull on the trigger.

How do you train to hit moving targets?

Practice, practice, practice. If you can't convince someone to run around (in protective gear of course) while you shoot at them, try to get somebody to toss objects in the air and let you try to hit them (the objects that is).

Can I use a player who's been killed to screen me from an opponent?

No, you can't use field officials or "dead men walking" to shield you from opposing players.

Is it considered a "hit" if a BB bounces off something and hits me?

A hit from a ricochet is not considered to be a good hit or "kill" shot. However, any BB that makes a direct hit on any part of you - canteen, hat, boot, whatever - is considered to be a kill shot.

Can I warn a teammate after I've been hit?

As soon as you've been hit you're considered to be "dead". Raise a hand to signal that you've been hit and go directly to the respawn area - don't say anything to any of your teammates.

What is a "bang" shot?
If you're within minimum engagement distance for your weapon, some games allow you to simply say something like "Bang, bang" in place of actually firing your weapon. Assuming you take your opponent by surprise and call "Bang, bang" first, that's considered a "kill" shot just as if you actually hit him with a BB.

What if there's someone on my team I can't stand?
There may come a time when you find yourself on a team with someone who wants to boss people around or who complains constantly or who blames you for his/her own mistakes. First of all, BE PATIENT -- people can change and airsoft games can teach even hard-headed people a few life lessons. Secondly, let your team leaders (if that's not you) deal with problem players. And third, try to grin and bear it. You're going to run into situations like this in the real world too and sometimes you just have to find a way to get along with people you don't like and work together to get the job done.

What if two teams are arguing during play and can't reach an agreement?
There's usually a field rule for this case where the two teams call for a time out or parlay and move off the field until the problem is resolved.

Should I practice running and shooting at the same time?
No, no one can shoot accurately while running. Practice MOVING and shooting at the same time. If you have to run, have one of your teammates provide covering fire rather than trying to do it yourself.

How do you prepare to go on patrol?
The basic steps involving in carrying out a patrol in an airsoft game are: meet with your team, work out a plan to achieve your objectives, rehearse the plan (as much as possible), begin executing the plan, revise the plan as it becomes necessary.

What are some things that will help a new player survive in game play?

Make sure you're in good physical condition. Airsoft game playing usually involves a considerable amount of physical activity. If you're not in decent shape you'll have a hard time keeping up. Don't be afraid to talk to your teammates when it's necessary - if you come under fire let your teammates know and give as much information as possible (direction of fire, etc.). If you're advancing on an enemy position and one of your people gets shot, hold up your advance and try to locate the shooter or shooters; don't keep moving forward without some idea of where the enemy fire is coming from. And strange as it may sound, don't be afraid to get shot - everyone does at times and it's one of the best ways to learn about what and what not to do. Also, don't hunker down in one place to try to avoid getting hit unless you're under heavy fire and in a protected position. In that case your best bet may be to sit tight and conserve your ammo until a counterattack or withdrawal can be organized.

Airsoft Resources

What is an airsoft game really like?

Here's an excerpt from a newspaper article that may give you a feeling for airsoft game play:

Gleason, Matt. "Combat Zone". Tulsa World. 11 June 2006:D1

These weekend warriors stalk each other with BB guns and learn about life.

William Sullivan, call sign Kashi, shoved the butt off his silenced, Maruzen APS-2 sniper rifle to   his right shoulder and prepared to fire. His enemies were out there.

The 17-year-old Kashistani sharpshooter with a ponytail and excellent marksmanship, wanted them dead.

Beyond Sullivan's dirt bunker lurked a nine-man special operations team, including one Brandon Robertson, call sign Pitt, a 28-year-old soldier known for tallying high body counts.

Robertson and company's assignment: rescue this captured reporter from the Kashistani bunker. Leave no survivors.

Sullivan, clad in Russian-issue camouflage and equipped with an AK-47 slung over his back and a Beretta pistol secured in a shoulder holster, didn't stand a chance of surviving, neither did his fellow Kashistani soldiers.

Of course, this was a war without bullets -- an airsoft war, a popular role-playing sport that originated in Asia before spreading to Europe, America and beyond.

And, yes, these guys take it all very seriously.

To read the entire article, go to:

http://www.tulsaworld.com/news/article.aspx?
no=subj&articleid=060611_Fa_D1_Comba23696&archive=yes

Are there any books on airsoft?

1) "Paintball and Airsoft Battle Tactics" by Christopher E. Larsen, John T. Gordon, and Hae-jung Larsen

2) "The Airsoft Legal Guide: Comprehensive Coverage on Airsoft Legal Matters" by MechboxPRO AirsoftPRESS

3) "Practical Airsoft Tactics: For Beginner: 2009 Edition" by MechboxPRO AirsoftPRESS

What are some good websites for airsoft articles and advice?
airsoftsociety.com, airsoftpress.com, WikiHow, airsoftfaqs.com, arniesairsoft.co.uk, airsoftretreat.com, fearphilippines.com

What are some good websites for airsoft videos?
Two of the best sites are www.youtube.com and www.mechbox.com. Mechbox in particular has some very good step-by-step videos on repairing, adjusting and upgrading airsoft guns. There are also a number of sites like www.airsoftpacific.com that have airsoft competition videos available for anyone who wants to get a look at what typical airsoft games are like.

The Gun Gallery

Here are a few of the actual firearms that have been produced as airsoft replicas of the real thing:

M1 (Garand):
The M1 Garand was the first semi-automatic rifle brought into general service by any country. It replaced the bolt-action Springfield M1903 as the standard issue rifle for the U.S. Infantry in 1936 and continued in that role through WW II and Korea until finally replaced by the M14 in 1957. The M1 actually continued to be used widely even after 1957, both by other countries (West Germany, Japan, and Italy) amd by U.S. Forces until finally going out of active service around 1965. The M1 is gas-operated, shoulder-fired, and fed by a clip holding eight .30-06 rounds. Unloaded, the M1 weighs around 10 pounds and has an effective range of around 400 meters (440 yards).

M1 Carbine:
The M1 carbine is a compact, light-weight, semi-automatic rifle that was used extensively by U.S. military forces in World War II and Korea. Initially intended for issue to support troops and some specialized units such as paratroopers, the M1 carbine eventually wound up in use by various front-line troops even though it had limited hitting power due to its use of a .30 caliber cartridge. The M1 spawned several variants including the M2 carbine (which offered full automatic fire capability) and the M3, which was basically an M2 outfitted with the "sniperscope" from the M1. The M1 and M2 carbines were eventually replaced by the M14 and later by the M16.

M14:
Last of the so-called "battle rifles", the M14 is a 7.62mm semi-auto/automatic weapon and served as the standard U.S. infantry rifle from 1959 to 1970. It's still in limited service today and was the basis for the M21 and M25 sniper rifles. The M14 was designed to take the place of four earlier rifles, the M1

Garand (standard U.S. infantry rifle in WWII), the M1 carbine, the M3, and the BAR (Browning Automatic Rifle). Partially because of the attempt to make the M14 a multi-purpose weapon it failed to measure up to the M1 Garand as an infantry rifle and was replaced by the M16 during the Vietnam war. There was some resistance to its retirement by troops who felt the M16 was an underpowered substitute for the M14, but by 1968-69 the M16A1 was fully deployed in Vietnam and proved to be a very capable weapon for insurgency warfare type situations.

Personal Note: I carried both the M14 and M16A1 and even though the M14 was almost impossible to control on full automatic, it is still my favorite rifle. And one place it was definitely superior to the M16 was in bayonet drills; try butt-stroking a bayonet dummy with an M16 and you're very likely to crack the plastic stock. However I do have to admit the lightweight M16 was much, much easier to lug around.

M16:

The M16 replaced the M14 as the standard U.S. infantry rifle in 1969-70. It's a lightweight, 5.56 mm, air-cooled, gas-operated, shoulder-fired weapon with a high muzzle velocity and a flat trajectory. The M16A4 is currently the newest model of the M16 and (along with the M4 carbine) is replacing the M16A2 as the U.S. military's standard assault rifle. The M16A4 has a flat-top receiver and four Picatinny rails for mounting a removable handgrip, sights, night vision devices, or a flashlight.

M21:

During Vietnam the U.S. Army decided it wanted an accurate, semi-automatic sniper rifle. In 1975, almost 1500 match grade M14s were fitted with a high-powered adjustable scope and designated as the M21 sniper rifle. The M21 served as the Army's primary sniper rifle from 1975 to 1988 until it was replaced by the M24 Sniper Weapon System.

M24:

The M24 Sniper Weapon System was developed to replace the stop-gap M21 (a modified version of the M14 infantry rifle). Developed by Remington, the M24 fires a 7.62mm NATO round from a 5 or 10-round internal magazine. It's a bolt-action rifle and has a muzzle velocity of around 2800 feet per second and features a stainless-steel barrel. Designed to withstand rough handling and battlefield conditions, the M24 has a removable bipod, a suppressor and a high-power sight that provides the M24 with an effective range of approximately 900 yards.

M25:

Built from a match grade M14, the M25 was designed to provide a long range rifle for use by Army Special Forces troops and Navy Seals. The M25 fulfills some specific needs for special forces units and is used as alternative to the M24 in certain situations. It's also referred to as the "White Feather", in honor of Carlos Hathcock, a legendary Marine sniper in Vietnam who always wore a white feather in his hat.

NOTE: Hathcock generally used a Winchester Model 70 .30-06 rifle and was credited with 93 confirmed kills. He also rescued seven Marines from a burning half-track when it struck a mine near Khe Sanh and then refused to accept a Silver Star for his actions, saying that anyone else would have done the same thing. Hathcock was so highly thought of by his fellow Marines that when the VC/NVA sent a platoon to hunt him down, many Marines in his area started wearing white feathers on their own bush hats to confuse the enemy snipers.

M40/M40A1/M40A3/M40A5:

The M40, M40A1, M40A3 and M40A5 are 7.62mm, bolt-action sniper rifles used by the U.S. Marine Corps. They use a 5-round detachable box magazine and are second cousins to the U.S. Army's M24 weapon system. Put into service in 1966, the different models of the M40 are all built around a Remington 700 and then modified by the Marine Corps. Maximum effective range is around 800 meters for all versions of the M40.

AK-47:

The AK-47 is a 7.62mm gas-operated assault rifle originally introduced into service in the Red Army in 1947 (the AK designation stands for "Avtomat Kalashnikova" or "Kalashnikov Automatic Rifle"). The AK-47 remains the most widely used and popular assault rifle in existence due to it's durability, ease of use, and low production cost. It has been manufactured and used by the military forces in many different countries all around the world. The biggest advantage of the AK-47 in combat is it's reliability; it's loose tolerances and rugged design allow it to absorb a good deal of punishment and continue to function. By the same token, its cheap construction makes it very inaccurate – it's basically a "spray and pray" weapon intended for use by unskilled troops.

Heckler and Koch G36:

The official assault rifle of the German army, the H&K G36 is a 5.56mm, gas-operated semi-automatic/automatic weapon that uses either a 30-round curved magazine or a 100-round drum magazine. It has a side-folding skeletonized stock and a detachable folding bipod. The standard German army version of the G36 has both a 3x telescopic sight and an unmagnified red-dot sight and it can also be fitted with an under-the-barrel grenade launcher. Like earlier H&K models, the G36 can be field-stripped and reassembled without tools by using a series of cross-pins.

Steyr AUG:

Designed in the 1970's by Steyr, Mannlicher GmbH & Company, the Steyr AUG is a 5.56mm bullpup assault rifle. It's the standard small arms rifle of the Austrian Army and is also in use by the Australian and Argentinian military. It's a selective-fire weapon (you pull the trigger half-way back for semi-automatic fire and all the way back for full automatic fire) and uses a double-column 30-round magazine. There's also a light machine gun version of the AUG that uses a 42-round magazine.

Thompson submachine gun (M1A1):

In 1938 the Thompson submachine gun was adopted by the U.S. Military and served during and after World War II. The M1A1 weighs around 11 pounds when empty and generally uses a 20 or 30 round box magazine. It has an effective range of 50 meters and fires .45 ACP (Automatic Colt Pistol) cartridges. The M1A1 Thompson became a favorite among troops in many countries (including the Viet Cong) because of its ability to deliver a high volume of short-range automatic weapons fire.

M1911A1:

For many years the M1911A1 (Colt .45) pistol was the standard sidearm for U.S. military forces. Originally put into service in 1911 as the M1911 it was re-designated as the M1911A1 after some minor external changes were made in 1924. It's a single-action, single-stack, magazine-fed and recoil-operated pistol chambered for the .45 ACP (Automatic Colt Pistol) round. After serving effectively in WW I, WW II, Korea and Vietnam, the M1911A1 was officially replaced by the Beretta 92FS in 1985. However, dissatisfaction with the stopping power of the Beretta's 9mm Parabellum round has kept the M1911A1 in service with many special operations units. In addition, several newer sidearms (such as the Heckler & Koch MK23) that also use the .45 ACP round have been adopted by certain special ops units.

Beretta M9:

The Beretta 92FS was adopted as the standard U.S. Sidearm in 1985 and designated the M9 pistol. The 92F is one of a series of similar pistols produced by Beretta, the Italian firearms manufacturer. The M9 fires a 9x19mm Parabellum cartridge and has a double-action first trigger pull, followed by a single-action pull for the remaining rounds. It's a semi-automatic, short recoil pistol and uses a 15-round staggered magazine. The M9 underwent some modification in 2006 and was re-designated as the M9A1, with the primary change being the addition of a Picatinny rail for attaching a flashlight, laser, or other accessories. The M9 weighs around two pounds and has an effective range of about 50 meters. Note: The U.S. Coast Guard has replaced the M9 with the SIG Sauer P229.

Appendix A - Glossary

134a: Least powerful propellant gas for airsoft guns

ACP: Automatic Colt Pistol

AAR: After Action Report

AEG: Automatic Electric Gun

AEP: Automatic Electric Pistol

Affirmative: OK or Yes

AK: "Avtomat Kalashnikova", Soviet rifle manufacturer

AO: Area of Operations

AR: Automatic Rifle

BAR: Browning Automatic Rifle (replaced by the M249 SAW)

BDU: Battle Dress Uniform

Breech: Housing a BB is moved into just before it's fired

Bump: slang for ambush

Bunny Hop: Tactic of jumping while moving to keep from being hit

Bullpup: A rifle where the firing mechanism and magazine are set behind the trigger and grip

C&C: Command and Control

Caliber: measure of the diameter of a bullet or BB

Camper: A player who stays in one position for a period of time

Carbine: Normally a shortened version of a particular rifle

CA: Classic Army (popular brand of airsoft guns)

Co2: Carbon dioxide gas, used as propellant for airsoft guns

CO: Commanding Officer

CONUS: Contiguous United States (doesn't include Alaska or Hawaii)

Check fire: check to make sure you're not firing at friendlies

Chronograph: device to measure BB speed

Cook: Wait time before throwing a grenade (to let the fuse burn down)

Clip: Term often mistakenly used in place of "magazine"; usually a metal strip used to fasten multiple rounds of ammunition together so they can be loaded into a magazine as a unit

CQB: Close Quarters Battle

CQC: Close Quarters Combat

DBDU: Desert Battle Dress Uniform (aka Chocolate Chip Camouflage uniform)

DE: Usually refers to a Desert Eagle pistol (Israeli made firearm)

DMR: Designated Marksman Rifle

EBB: Electric Blow Back (type of blowback pistol or rifle)

FA: Forward Area (area where contact with the enemy is most likely)

FARP: Fueling and Rearming Point

FEBA: Forward Edge of Battle Area

FF: Friendly Fire

Flank: Area to the right or left of a unit's position

FLS: Field Landing Strip

FM: Usually refers to a military Field Manual

FOV: Field of View

Frag: Fragmentation grenade

FPS: Feet per second

FTL: Fire Team Leader

FTX: Field Training Exercise

Gearbox (Mechbox): The firing mechanism on an AEG

GBB: Gas Blow Back (type of blowback pistol or rifle that simulates the blow back of an actual firearm)

GPS: Global Positioning System

Green Gas: Type of propellant used for airsoft guns

HE: High Explosive

HMG: Heavy Machine Gun

Hi-Cap: High Capacity Magazine

Hop-Up: A device built into many airsoft guns to increase range

HK or H&K: Heckler and Koch, German gun manufacturer

HQ: Headquarters

IAD: Immediate Action Drill

ICF: I Chih Shivan Enterprises (airsoft manufacturer)

IMI: Israeli Military Industries

IDF: Israeli Defense Forces

Joule: A measure of energy, often used as a measurement of the power of a particular airsoft gun.

KWC: Kine Well Company (airsoft manufacturer)

LAM: Light Accessory Module

LAW: Light Antitank Weapon

LMG: Light Machine Gun

LOF: Line of Fire

LOS: Line of Sight

LPEG: Low Power Electric Gun (generally considered a "beginner gun")

LZ: Landing Zone

M11A1: Mac 11

M16A1 or M16A2: standard issue rifle for the United States Army

M4: 14.5" barrel carbine version of the M16A2

M4A1: Modified version of the M4 (includes full auto fire)

M203: Grenade launcher attachment for the M16A2 and M4A1

M249: Squad Automatic Weapon (SAW); provides heavy fire support for an infantry squad

M24: Standard marksman rifle for U.S. Army

M82A1: Barrett rifle, semi-automatic marksman rifle (U.S. Army)

M9: 9mm Beretta handgun, standard sidearm for U.S. Army

MP5: Popular H&K submachine gun

Mag: Magazine

MaH: Milliamp Hours (rating system for batteries)

MARS: Multipurpose Aiming Reflex Sight

MED: Minimum Engagement Distance

MEU: Marine Expeditionary Unit

MG: Machine gun

MILES: Multiple Integrated Laser Engagement System (used in combat simulations)

MilSim: Military Simulation

MOUT: Military Operations in Urban Terrain

MPEG: Medium Power Electric Gun

MWS: Modular Weapon System

NBB: Non Blow Back

NCO: Noncommissioned Officer (rank of corporal or above)

Negative: No

NVD: Night Vision Device

OP: Observation Post

OPFOR: Opposing Forces

OPORD: Operation Order (mission plan)

ORP: Objective Rally Point

P90: Submachine gun (Made by FN)

PDW: Personal Defense Weapon (compact defensive weapon like the FN P90)

Picatinny: Type of rail system for mounting accessories (scopes, flashlights, etc.) on a gun

PLT: Platoon

POW: Prisoner of War

Red Gas: powerful gas propellant for airsoft guns

R.I.S.: Rail Interface System (for mounting accessories on a gun)

ROE: Rules of Engagement (rules for how, when and where you are allowed to engage the enemy)

RPG: Rocket Propelled Grenade

RPM: Rounds per Minute

ROF: Rate of Fire (rounds per minute)

SAW: Squad Automatic Weapon (see M249)

SF: Special Forces

SITREP: Situation Report

Smoke: Smoke grenade

Slide: Generally, the top half of a semi-automatic pistol

SQD: Squad (generally 8 to 12 soldiers)

SMG: Sub Machine Gun

SPAS: Special Purpose Automatic Shotgun

Stock: The rear end of a rifle, the part that fits against your shoulder

UIF: Unidentified Indigenous Forces

UHC: Unicorn Hobby Company

Weaver Rail: rail that fits on a weapon, used to attach scopes, etc.

Zeroing: Adjusting the sights on your gun so your shots land on target

Appendix B – Game Tips

Before the game starts be sure to secure anything you're carrying that might clank or rattle as you move.

Make sure you know the effective range of your weapon or weapons (which may vary with the temperature). It's pointless and a waste of ammo to start shooting at someone who's out of range.

When you're playing on a large outdoor game field try to make a map of the area ahead of time so you have some idea of the terrain and obstacles you'll encounter during the game.

If you spot a group of enemy troops, be careful rushing to come up behind them - they may have left a couple of "sleepers" trailing them to protect their rear.

Once you've fired at someone move to a different position - odds are that you've been spotted.

If enemy troops are closing in on you, it may help to try the unexpected. See if you can head directly toward them and sneak past them.

If you're taken hostage (assuming your game allows for hostages) take note of exactly where you're being held. If you can escape you may be able to pinpoint where the enemy's command center is located.

Firing an AEG continuously on full automatic can end up stripping the gears or overheating the motor.

If you're exchanging fire with opposing players who are pretty well concealed, you may want to have everyone on your side stop firing for a couple of minutes. That may be enough to convince the guys on the other side that you've pulled back, run out of ammo or whatever and get them to break cover.

In general you don't want to stay in one place too long during a game. However, if you're really good at using camouflage and cover you may be able to sit tight for a while, pick off a couple of passing enemy troops, then move to a new position and do the same thing again.

It's a good idea to carry a sidearm in case your AEG, shotgun or sniper rifle malfunctions in the middle of a battle. Your best bet is an AEP (Automatic Electric Pistol) or a gas operated pistol.

If you're pinned down by a sniper, try throwing something in one direction to distract the sniper while you move in a different direction.

Don't use cheap BBs in your weapon - use only seamless, highly polished BBs. Cheap, unevenly finished BBs can damage the inside of your barrel and cause your gun to jam.

Don't bunch together; maintain an interval of a few feet between each team member if at all possible (without losing the ability to communicate with each other).

For longer games be sure to carry plenty of water with you to avoid dehydration.

Look in the swimming supplies section of your local discount store for anti-fog drops; use them to keep your goggles from fogging up during a game.

If you're close to a member of your team who gets hit, get away from there - when your teammate calls out that he's been hit, the other side may concentrate fire on that location.

If you are responsible for covering a certain area, don't automatically turn your head if you hear firing from some other direction; stay focused on your area.

Remember that long rifles make it hard to turn and move quickly in tight spaces, such as CQB game layouts.

For a game with a large number of players scattered over a

wide area it's helpful for your team to wear a certain color armband to avoid shooting one of your own people.

If enemy troops are hiding in a building and you can't think of any good way to get to them, try waiting them out for a while. If they get bored and start to leave the building, attack them when they're out in the open.

Conserve your ammo - don't fire BBs just to be shooting. If you don't have a good target, wait till you do. After all, if you use up all your BBs and suddenly find yourself under attack, you're going to wish you had those wasted BBs back.

If you're finished shooting, then after you remove the magazine from your gun fire one shot to make sure the chamber's empty - don't leave "one in the pipe".

If you're defending a building in a CQB game, try fastening obstacles in doorways at about knee height (making sure that they're visible enough that no one is going to fall over them). Having to step up and over the obstacle can be awkward for attackers and make them more vulnerable as they come through the doorway.

Charging or rushing the enemy is usually just a good way to get "killed". As a rule, don't try rushing your opponents unless you definitely have the advantage of surprise or a major advantage in numbers.

If you've decided to buy a better airsoft gun and aren't sure which one to get, other airsofters are usually willing to let you try out their weapon. Just remember to ask politely and make sure you know how to operate the gun so you don't damage it.

Remember not to wear anything shiny or reflective. Things like a bright metal belt buckle or dog tags can catch the sun and give away your position. Also, something that may be important if you're trying to move absolutely silently -- a pair of dog tags worn loose around your neck can actually clink together and make an audible sound. You can get rubber "silencers" to fit around the dog tags to keep that from happening.

Unless you're expecting enemy contact at any second, never move quickly with your finger actually on the trigger -- it's too easy to fire your weapon accidentally. Keep your finger extended, laying alongside the trigger but not actually curled around it.

Don't use silicon spray on your gun right before a game. It reduces the friction on the BBs as they travel through the barrel (for about the first 100 to 200 shots) so your hop-up setting will be off and your BBs won't land on target.

Never put your hand, face or any part of your body directly in front of the muzzle of a loaded airsoft gun.

If you're more than 50 feet away from an opponent, try to hit him more than once -- at greater distances a single hit may go unnoticed.

Be sure to clean your gun after every game. Wipe it down with a clean rag and make sure you clean the barrel. Also, remember to clean off any magazine that happened to hit the ground during the game.

Never dip your airsoft gun in water to wash it off - wipe it down with a clean rag or with cotton swabs (slightly dampened if necessary).

To estimate how many shots you can get from your AEG with a fully charged battery, check your battery's maH (milliamp hours) rating and figure that you'll get one shot for each maH.

If you're in a firefight and sprinting to a new position, it doesn't hurt to fire a few rounds towards the enemy while you're moving. You probably won't get a hit, but it may get them to duck or dive for cover - which gives you a better chance of not getting hit.

Always wear a long-sleeved shirt and full-length pants for game play; even a plastic BB can sting or leave a welt if it hits bare skin. Just be sure you don't wear so much heavy clothing that you can't feel if you've been hit.

If at all possible, maintain a reserve force that can react to changing conditions.

Appendix C – Airsoft Vendors

Here are a few of the more highly recommended websites where you can purchase airsoft guns, equipment and supplies:

www.airsoftgi.com

www.airsoftextreme.com

www.airsoftatlanta.com

www.evike.com (occasional problems with not updating stock – items show as in stock when they are not – you wind up with items on backorder)

www.airsoftmegastore.com

www.shortyusa.com (somewhat higher prices than other sites)

www.pyramydairsoft.com (very reliable although not as wide a selection as some sites)

www.redwolfairsoft.com (good site, fairly high shipping if outside the U.K.)

Printed in Great Britain
by Amazon